Mission-Focused Congregations

A Bible Study

Lois Barrett, editor

Faith & Life Resources

A Division of Mennonite Publishing House
Scottdale, Pennsylvania
Newton, Kansas
Waterloo, Ontario
Winnipeg, Manitoba
1 800 245-7894 or 1 800 743-2484
www.mph.org

The paper used in this publication is recycled and meets the minimum requirements of American National Standard for Information Sciences—Permanence of Paper for Printed Library Materials, ANSI Z39.48-1984.

MISSION-FOCUSED CONGREGATIONS: A BIBLE STUDY

Published simultaneously in Canada by Faith & Life Resources, Waterloo, Ont. N2L 6H7
International Standard Book Number: 0-8361-9212-5
Printed in the United States of America
Book and cover design by Gwen M. Stamm
Website: www.mph.org

Contents

Introduction

THIS BIBLE STUDY is about the nature of the church. It is the conviction of those who prepared this study (1) that the church can only be defined around its participation in God's mission in the world and its living into God's future that has already begun, and (2) that what God is doing in the world is setting things right, redeeming and restoring all things in Christ to God's intended design. This understanding of the church is what we call the "missional church."

This study will not give you five easy steps to becoming a missional church. There are no such five easy steps. This is not a course on how to get more members on the church rolls. This is not a book on how to have more service projects. The purpose of this study is (1) to provide a fuller definition of "missional church" through careful examination of the New Testament and (2) to inspire congregations and small groups to see themselves as missional, both in what they do and in who they are.

The Bible study method reflected in each of the seven sessions is the missional method. When we are a missional church we are paying attention to (1) context, (2) God's action, and (3) our participation in what God is doing. Therefore we begin each Bible study with attention to **context**. What is the context of the biblical passage? What in

Being a missional church includes how we live our lives together as a congregation before the watching world. Our being needs to match our doing.

the biblical context is like our context? Where are we? What is our world like?

Second, we pay attention to the **gospel**. What is God doing in this world? In the biblical text, where was God at work? What was God's good news? Where can we see God at work? How do we hear God's good news? How does God call us to change? How does God challenge us to enter the reign of God?

Third, we pay attention to the **church**. How is God calling and sending us to participate in God's mission in the world? How does the biblical text call the church to proclaim the reign of God by word and deed? How does this text call and send the church, in all of its life together, to be a sign of the reign of God? What are the next steps for our group or our congregation? How can everything we do be more oriented around God's mission in the world?

Quotations, teaching helps, discussion questions, and instructions to the leader are included in each lesson in the narrow column. Biblical quotations are from the New Revised Standard Version (NRSV).

In the course of these Bible studies, we believe you will see that being a missional church involves much more than the missions committee, the witness commission, or what is done outside the church walls. Being a missional church includes how we live our lives together as a congregation before the watching world. Our being needs to match our doing.

About the writers

Plans for this study began in the conversation between Faith & Life Resources, Mennonite Publishing House, and the "Becoming a Missional Church" Project Team of the Mennonite mission transition process. Others were drawn into the conversation as well. Several contributors agreed to prepare this book. Their names and church related responsibilities at the time of writing were as follows.

Lois Barrett, executive secretary of the Commission on Home Ministries, General Conference Mennonite Church, Newton, Kansas.

Gilberto Flores, director of Hispanic Resource Ministries for the Commission on Home Ministries, Newton, Kansas.

James Krabill, vice-president for Mission Advocacy and Communication for Mennonite Board of Missions, Elkhart, Indiana.

J. Nelson Kraybill, president of Associated Mennonite Biblical Seminary, Elkhart, Indiana.

Linford Stutzman, associate professor of Culture and Mission at Eastern Mennonite Seminary, Harrisonburg, Virginia.

Robert J. Suderman, executive secretary of the Ministries Commission, Mennonite Church Canada, Winnipeg, Manitoba.

Suggested leadership plan for study, discussion, and action

1. Read the story at the beginning of the session.
2. Then read the Scripture passages.

Context—Where are we?

Use the questions in the "for discussion" sections of the session. Or create your own questions about the connections between the biblical context and our context. What in our context is like the biblical context?

Gospel—What is God doing?

Use the questions in the "for discussion" sections or ask your own questions about what God is doing in the Scripture passage and what God is doing in our context.

Church—How is God calling and sending us to participate in God's mission in the world?

Again, use the questions in the "for discussion" sections or ask your own questions. (See sample questions in the introduction.)

End each session with a time of prayer for God's help in being a missional church.

SESSION 1

God's mission in the world

Robert J. Suderman

I REMEMBER Juan and Pedro (names have been changed). We had been working together as members of the executive committee of an emerging Hispanic group in our congregation. This group was made up of persons fleeing from dangers in their own countries in Latin America who had been accepted as refugees in our country. Most of them came from Central America where civil war was rampant.

The group had elected this committee to envision and plan activities. We had been meeting regularly for six months. Both Juan and Pedro were active and enthusiastic members of the committee. Both had told me privately of some of their background activities and the details of the events that forced them to flee and seek refuge. They represented the opposite ends of the political and ideological spectrum. Essentially, they had been enemies. It was also clear to me that, in the dynamics of the group, it was difficult to build enough trust to share each other's lives openly.

I joyfully participated in an unfolding miracle. Week after week, former members and sympathizers of the *Sandinistas* and the *Contras* from Nicaragua were gathered around the open Word of God, singing and praying together. There were those from the revolutionary forces of Guatemala and El Salvador. There were Chileans who had fled the persecution of Pinochet.

The differences among the gathered community were extreme.

It reminded me of Jesus' attempt to form a community from Zealots and tax collectors. Trust among them developed slowly while conflicts could erupt frequently. Each had their own story of how they had become committed to the Mennonite church and why they had sought out a Mennonite church in their new home. Each story was a miracle of prayer, action, hospitality, and providence.

Yet there were many things they didn't know about each other and were unwilling to share about themselves. There was fear that the long arms of the revolutions and wars left behind would somehow reach into their new communities and homes. Full disclosure was too big a risk.

In one of our meetings, while talking about their backgrounds, Pedro inadvertently let slip a former nickname that he had carried in his home country. There were a few more questions about geography and approximate location of his previous activity. Then there was an interesting silence. Juan warily asked whether Pedro had ever visited a certain cooperative farm. Pedro stated that he had been there frequently because he was their supplier of ——. "Are you [nickname]?" asked Juan. "Yes, I am. And who are you?" asked Pedro. "I was [nickname]," answered Juan. "I was the buyer of ——." Juan and Pedro jumped off their chairs and fell into a long and emotional embrace. Tears streamed down their faces. After a long while, we sat down and began to reconstruct the story. Each described the other in his former life. They used to have long beards, hats low over their eyebrows, dark sunglasses, and long, flowing, dirty hair. Both had carried guns, holsters, and other weapons. They had known each other only by nicknames. Although they had been enemies, they had some common needs. They had met each other frequently, taken care of "business" briskly, and continued in their separate ways.

Here they found themselves sitting on the same executive committee in a Mennonite church. Their hair was cut, the uniforms were gone, and weapons had been left behind. The contrast could not have been greater, and no one understood this better than they did. This encounter changed the dynamics of the group.

They told their wives and families. They shared with the group. Our study of the Sermon on the Mount took on new urgency and energy for everybody. We were witnesses to the transforming power of the gospel to change lives, to give new meaning to families, and to find sustenance for a journey into a new life. We experienced the miracle of the power of the gospel to reconcile former enemies. There was a new world for them. Former things were seen through different glasses. Lenses were changed. In every way, there was a "new creation."

Biblical text

2 Corinthians 5:16–6:2

> [16] From now on, therefore, we regard no one from a human point of view; even though we once knew Christ from a human point of view, we know him no longer in this way. [17] So if anyone is in Christ, there is a new creation: everything old has passed away; see, everything has become new! [18] All this is from God, who reconciled us to himself through Christ, and has given us the ministry of reconciliation; [19] that is, in Christ God was reconciling the world to himself, not counting their trespasses against them, and entrusting the message of reconciliation to us. [20] So we are ambassadors for Christ, since God is making his appeal through us. We entreat you on behalf of Christ, be reconciled to God. [21] For our sake he made him to be sin who knew no sin, so that in him we might become the righteousness of God.
>
> [1] As we work together with him, we urge you also not to accept the grace of God in vain. [2] For he says,
> "At an acceptable time I have listened to you,
> And on the day of salvation I have helped you."
> See, now is the acceptable time; see now is the day of salvation!

A challenge

The apostle Paul is encouraging the church in Corinth to consider its vocation in its context. Let's highlight some of the importance emphases in this passage.

1. God is the initiator, author, and sustainer of mission.

Note the following:

- All this is from God. . . .
- [God] through Christ reconciled us to himself. . . .
- [God] gave us the ministry of reconciliation. . . .
- God was in Christ reconciling the world to himself. . . .
- [God] entrusted to us the message of reconciliation. . . .
- God makes his appeal through us. . . .
- Be reconciled to God. . . .
- Become the righteousness of God. . . .
- Work together with [God]. . . .
- God's grace must not be accepted in vain. . . .
- [God] establishes the acceptable time and the day of salvation. . . .

God is the first missionary. God works in many ways, but especially through the saving presence of Jesus Christ. While the church is invited in, it is not the author of mission.

2. God works at reconciliation.

Note the following:

- [God] reconciled us to himself. . . .
- God was in Christ reconciling the world to himself. . . .
- [God] gave us the ministry of reconciliation. . . .
- [God] entrusted us with the ministry of reconciliation. . . .
- As ambassadors of God, on behalf of Christ, we plead with you to be reconciled. . . .

It is instructive that the meaning of the root word *reconciliation* in the Greek language is the word "catalyst" or catalase *(katallasso)*. A catalyst is a substance that energizes and speeds up change in other things without being changed itself. For example, catalase, when in contact with hydrogen peroxide, converts the hydrogen to water and frees the oxygen from the substance. Catalase facilitates this without itself undergoing change. This is a marvelous description of the work of God's Spirit through Christ: The Spirit transforms, converts, and sets free without its own character and intention ever changing.

And the church is called and sent to be a messenger, a minister, an ambassador of this transforming and freeing work of God. What an invitation! What a privilege!

3. The church is invited to be a "co-worker" *(sunergos)* with God (6:1).

To be considered a co-worker with God may seem tame to us. But such an affirmation coming from the apostle Paul, a Jewish Pharisee, would have been blasphemous in his time. God's holiness was such that it was presumptuous to think of humans as co-workers with God. Yes, God worked with his people (Romans 8:28). Or people could be co-workers with people (Romans 16:3, 9, 21). But it was highly unusual to classify people as co-workers with God. Only three times is this suggested in the New Testament, each time by the apostle Paul (compare 1 Corinthians 3:9; 1 Thessalonians 3:2; 2 Corinthians 6:1). It is important for us to sense again the scandalous nature of what Paul is proposing. To be invited, as a co-worker, into the reconciling work of God is a very high honor for the church.

4. In Christ, there is a new creation.

The translation of 2 Corinthians 5:17 in the NRSV says: "If anyone is in Christ, *there is* a new *creation*." We should note two important differences from other translations:

• The word often translated as "creature" *(ktisis)* is here translated "creation."

Mission is the crossing of a frontier of strangeness between faith in Christ as Lord and unbelief in order to make Christ known and obeyed as Lord among those who do not know and obey Him.

—Leslie Newbigin, *One Body, One Gospel, One World: The Christian Mission Today* (London: International Missionary Council, 1958), p. 29.

• The subject and verb of the second clause are "there is" instead of "he is," as in many other translations.

The reason for these shifts is that the text in Greek actually has no subject or verb in the second clause. In the Greek text it appears simply as an exclamation: "If anyone is in Christ—NEW CREATION!" The focus of this text is not really on what happens "inside the person" who is in Christ, important as that may be. The focus is more on what happens to the creation when viewed from the perspective of reconciliation in Christ. The NRSV has captured this element of surprise: " . . . there is a NEW CREATION!" The world really does look different when it is experienced and viewed through the eyes of Christ's reconciling work.

5. We no longer see the world from "human" (*sarx:* literally, flesh, bodily) perspectives.

"We regard no one from a human point of view." Reconciliation in Christ means that we perceive creation from a godly perspective. What does our neighbor look like through the lenses of reconciliation in Christ? What does war look like? What does poverty look like? What do family life and marriage look like? Paul's suggestion that reconciliation really does generate a "new creation" is clearly demonstrated in the story of Juan and Pedro. It is amazing how different things look when we respond to the reconciliation offered to us by God in Christ. It truly is the "acceptable time . . . the day of salvation" when these new lenses are offered and received.

For discussion

a. How does the story of Juan and Pedro illustrate the text from 2 Corinthians? What similar stories can you tell from your experiences?
b. Take a careful look at how the word *reconciliation* is defined in this passage. What does this imply for the ministry of the church? What might it mean for the church to be a catalyst of reconciliation?

c. Share some stories about how the creation seems new when experienced through our reconciliation with God through Christ.
d. What examples can you give of the difference between the human point of view and seeing creation through the perspective of reconciliation?

Context—Where are we?

Corinth was a bustling city of commerce and crafts, situated on a key trade route between Asia Minor and Italy. It was a wealthy city. Corinth attracted artisans, entrepreneurs, foreigners, people from the Orient, and "freedmen" who wanted to make their mark in the plentiful commercial possibilities.

The social milieu of the bustling city is also reflected in the emerging church of Corinth. There was energy, diversity, and entrepreneurship in the church. There were leadership, authority, and power struggles in the congregation (1 Corinthians 1:12ff.; 3:3-9). Paul's authority was under severe criticism (1 Corinthians 15:3-11; 7:40; 2 Corinthians 12:12) and he, in turn, addressed the would-be leaders in sarcastic tones with considerable rhetoric (2 Corinthians 10-13).

It is evident that some "super-apostles" had come into the congregation and caused some severe conflict and division. There were the "strong" and the "weak," the rich and the poor, the Jews and the Greeks (1 Corinthians 10–11). There were the spiritualists and those who criticized the ones who spoke in tongues (1 Corinthians 14). There were those who wanted to interrupt and take over the worship services and those who advocated for more order (1 Corinthians 11, 14). There were prophets, both male and female, and there were varieties of conflicting sexual, dress, and behavior codes at work in the same group (1 Corinthians 7, 11). There were those who did not understand the meaning of the resurrection (1 Corinthians 15), and misused the supper for commemorating Jesus' death and resurrection (1 Corinthians 11). The aggressive entrepreneurial spirit so evident in the city was clearly at work in the congregation as well.

Gospel—What is God doing?

To this group Paul addresses his vision that they are ambassadors of reconciliation. They have been reconciled in Christ, and have now been invited to share in the ministry of reconciliation. In this passage, the good news (gospel) can be seen in that:

- Reconciliation is possible, even in this group, because it doesn't depend on them; it is initiated by God.
- Christ redeems and changes the ordinary lives of people because it is the Spirit of God at work in them.
- God anoints an undeserving people to be his ambassadors in the world.
- These people reflect both the power of God's reconciling initiative and the potential of becoming instruments for reconciliation.
- The church is empowered to be more than it already is in Corinth (and in the rest of the world).
- This is a "new day," the acceptable time of God, the time in which we to live now.

Church—How is God calling and sending?

This passage shows that God is a reconciler. God is a catalyst, forever changing and transforming things without being changed himself. The text further states that this reconciliation is done through Christ, through the ambassadorship of the church, and with the world.

Today, our world too is in desperate need of reconciliation with God. To understand our need for reconciliation, we need only mention phrases like: marriage breakdown, family disintegration, alienation and loneliness, international foreign policy, globalization of corporate power, war, capital punishment, poverty, revolution, strikes, and suicide rates. Each one of us experiences some need for reconciliation. None of us is excluded or isolated from the needs within and around us.

What would happen if we understood that the purpose of God is reconciliation? Let's imagine for a moment that "reconciling the world with himself" is in fact the primary activity of God in the world. Let's imagine that the church is invited into this activity as co-workers with God. And let's further imagine that the church understands that it need not and should not define its own purposes in the world beyond the basic purpose of God. The reconciling ambassadorship task is the reason the church exists. And let's imagine that we understand how Jesus Christ is central to this reconciling function, and that we have committed ourselves to be faithful in this vocation that we have been called for and sent into.

What would happen? Let's imagine:

- The church would be actively seeking places where reconciliation is urgently needed. This search, surely, would take the church into the lives of individuals, families, communities, neighborhoods, regions, races, religions, and nations.
- In the process of actively seeking such places, the church would grow in its understanding of the context in which we live and minister.
- The church would try to discern how God is already present in those places, working at reconciling each situation to himself through Jesus Christ.
- Such understanding would surely lead the church to deeper study, meditation, reflection, worship, and prayer.
- The church would direct all of its energy and resources to align each activity and member with this purpose. This alignment would include everything from the ushers to the finance committee, Sunday school curriculum to pastoral training, worship to children's clubs.
- The church would be involved in community issues and respond in solidarity to places where reconciliation is sought.
- The church would be a reconciled community and would actively and excitedly invite others to join such a good experience.
- The church would seek ways of understanding how the teachings and ministry of Jesus could become central to those who do not yet know about them, and invite others to consider Jesus as their life and guide.

In short, the church would be missional. Its spirit and activities would be aligned with the Spirit and the activity of God in the world. The church would be faithful to its calling and purpose. It would be a community contrasting with communities that have other priorities and purposes. The church would be salt and light. It would be a city on a hill. It would be an oasis in the desert. The church's presence and ministry would be relevant to the issues swimming all around us. The church would speak a Word of God to the world seeking direction. All in all, the church would be the church.

For discussion

a. Review the description of a missional church. Is your congregation "missional" in the sense that it is defined here? What things could be changed to make it more so?
b. What commitments or suggestions could your study group make so that your congregation would function as a fully missional congregation?

SESSION 2

Jesus sends the church

J. Nelson Kraybill

Being sent when we're afraid

Bloodstains were still on the pavement when members of Prairie Street Mennonite Church, Elkhart, Indiana, gathered to pray at the street where a seventeen-year-old boy had been stabbed to death a few days earlier. It was the third murder in our small city within a week, a reminder of the violence and fear in neighborhoods where unemployment and drug use are daily realities. Ironically, the stains marred the words "Caution Children" painted on the pavement.

An elder in the congregation declared the murder spot "holy ground." Together we committed that place of brokenness to the healing power of God. "In the name of Jesus Christ we bind the powers of sin and death that destroy and kill. We claim this street for Christ, and pray that no violence will ever happen here again."

It's spiritually and emotionally unnerving to be close to brutal death. But most of us who gathered to pray that morning could slip away to the haven of our homes in better parts of the city. We could go to our places of study or employment where violence is not a daily threat. A purse snatching did occur recently inside our church building on a Sunday morning. But our weekly worship services usually feel pretty secure and insulated from the poverty and the needs so close by in tenant housing.

"Peace be with you. As the Father has sent me, so I send you" (John 20:21). Could we who just visited a murder scene hear the risen Christ speak those words to us? What does it mean for us to be sent into a world where there is fear and danger?

Biblical text

John 20:19-23

> [19] When it was evening on that day, the first day of the week, and the doors of the house where the disciples had met were locked for fear of the Jews, Jesus came and stood among them and said, "Peace be with you." [20] After he said this, he showed them his hands and his side. Then the disciples rejoiced when they saw the Lord. [21] Jesus said to them again, "Peace be with you. As the Father has sent me, so I send you." [22] When he had said this, he breathed on them and said to them, "Receive the Holy Spirit. [23] If you forgive the sins of any, they are forgiven them; if you retain the sins of any, they are retained."

Context: A huddle of scared disciples—Where are we?

On the first resurrection Sunday, a band of frightened disciples of Jesus gathered at a home in Jerusalem. No wonder they locked the doors. They had just witnessed the brutal death of their teacher and Lord—and knew they could be next for execution. The Roman philosopher Cicero said crucifixion was such a hideous means of death that "the very word 'cross' should be far removed" from the eyes and thoughts of Roman citizens. Crucifixion was an agonizing and heartless death reserved for slaves, traitors, and despised foreigners.

A few women among the disciples actually had the courage to stay with Jesus at the crucifixion site until he died. The men—except for the "beloved disciple" (John 19:25-27)—had run for their lives. Now in the locked house in Jerusalem there must have been a confused mass of feelings and emotions: fear for their own safety, shame at having abandoned Jesus, and confusion about life's purpose now that Jesus was gone.

Adding to the chaos was an electrifying rumor. A few women among Jesus' followers reported having seen him alive. But their story may not have convinced many fellow disciples. Cultures of the Roman Empire usually did not give women as much power or credibility as men. The testimony of women in the ancient world was not considered reliable enough to stand up in court. In this case it was Mary Magdalene who announced Jesus' resurrection (John 20:18)—a woman so troubled that Jesus had cast seven demons from her (Mark 16:9). Had the demons returned, convincing her she saw a dead man walking? Probably most of the disciples were as skeptical as Thomas: "Unless I see the mark of the nails in his hands . . . I will not believe" (John 20:25).

More than skepticism, though, it was raw *fear* that confined Jesus' disciples in a huddle behind locked doors. John says they barricaded themselves "for fear of the Jews" (20:19). Of course, the disciples themselves were Jewish. Perhaps John means they feared Jewish religious *leaders*, some of whom had cooperated with Roman authorities in the arrest and execution of Jesus. But the disciples of Jesus also may have feared ridicule and contempt from Jewish neighbors, friends, and family members. Why had the disciples been so gullible as to believe Jesus' claims about arrival of the kingdom of God and his own divine authority? Had they abandoned the security of jobs and home for a false messiah?

Context: When we stay behind closed doors—Where are we?

There are places in the world today where Christians huddle in secret because they fear for their lives. But in North America, if disciples of Jesus keep our faith behind closed doors, it probably has more to do with fear of change or fear of being labeled overzealous. Whatever our ethnic or economic group, we are most likely to feel comfortable with people similar to ourselves. It would take time and energy to learn to know new neighbors from a different ethnic background. We would have to change schedule priorities and shift our patterns of friendship to include new nationalities or new racial and economic groups in our church.

Beyond the fear of needing to change relationship patterns is the fear that our confession of Christ as Lord might not be received as good news. Gone are the days when a majority of North Americans are familiar with Christian values and beliefs. A growing number of people have no religious framework at all for their lives—even though they may pursue financial security or entertainment with near-religious zeal. Others put together a tossed salad of beliefs, creating their own mix of understandings from a supermarket of world religions.

With religious faith now private and individualistic in North America, we may hesitate to make confident claims about the lordship of Jesus Christ. Pressure from surrounding culture squeezes us into thinking that Jesus is *a* way to God, not *the* way. We may be ashamed to share our conviction that Jesus is the Son of God in a sense that no other religion can claim. We may be silent about our certainty that the resurrection was a turning point in human history, that Jesus someday will return to renew all of creation. We may want to quietly go about our work and family life—including regular worship at church—but be afraid to speak or act in ways that tell the world we are followers of Jesus.

For discussion

a. Why do you think the disciples were afraid?

b. Can you identify with the doubts and demands of Thomas?

c. Name the reasons Christians in North America might want to keep our faith behind closed doors. Why might we be afraid?

d. Do you know stories of Christians from North America or elsewhere in the world who needed to survive and give witness in circumstances of physical danger? What sustains and empowers believers in such settings?

Gospel: A peace that touches all areas of life—What is God doing?

"Peace be with you" (John 20:21) were the first words Jesus spoke to the huddle of scared disciples. These also are words for the church today. Both in the ancient and the modern world, peace often means little more than absence of war. But Jesus, drawing from a long tradition of *shalom* (peace) in Hebrew thought, gives this word rich meaning. In both Jewish and Christian thought, peace includes well being, justice, restored relationships, and an end to violence.

When Jesus said, "Peace be with you," he calmed the agitated emotions of frightened followers. But if this blessing started with internal calm, it meant much more than that. In Jesus' ministry, peace was a condition of being healed (Mark 5:34) or forgiven (Luke 7:50). It also spilled over into confrontations in society: followers of Jesus are peace*makers* (Matthew 5:9; Colossians 1:20) who put away the sword (John 18:36).

How we are tempted to keep peace for ourselves! It is natural to want to create an island of calm and good relationships within church or family—and ignore the broken world beyond our daily routine. We struggle enough sometimes to keep peace in our homes and congregations, and don't have energy or time to be peacemakers in the world.

But Jesus immediately connects peace to mission: "Peace be with you. As the Father has sent me, so I send you"(John 20:21). How often has the church separated mission and evangelism from peacemaking? Sometimes we assign people to one camp or another—"evangelicals" who invite others to believe in Jesus and "peace people" who oppose military spending or work against racism. But a commitment to peace between God and mortals cannot be separated from moving out into the world as peacemakers and evangelists.

Gospel: Witness empowered by the Holy Spirit—What is God doing?

Jesus knew that bold witness and authentic peacemaking were daunting tasks. Already, before his death, Jesus promised that he would not leave his followers "orphaned" (John 14:18) for the work ahead. Jesus assured the disciples that the Holy Spirit, "whom the Father will send in my name, will teach you everything, and remind you of all that I have said to you. Peace I leave with you" (John 14:26-27).

Now, in his first resurrection appearance to the gathered band of disciples, Jesus "breathed on them"(John 20:22). This reminds the disciples of the breath (Spirit) of God in the Genesis story of creation. Through Christ, God is creating a new people—and soon a "new heaven and a new earth" (Revelation 21:1). God's mission is nothing less than "to reconcile to himself all things" (Colossians 1:20).

"Receive the Holy Spirit," Jesus declared. "If you forgive the sins of any, they are forgiven them; if you retain the sins of any, they are retained" (John 20:22-23). It is the Holy Spirit that empowers the church for an integrated witness of peacemaking and forgiveness of sin. The Holy Spirit *reminds us of what Jesus taught*, pointing us to the Sermon on the Mount and other places where Jesus shows us how to live by standards of the kingdom of God.

"The failure of Christians to live according to the standards of the Sermon on the Mount does not absolve them from the challenge to do so. Particularly in our contemporary world of violence and counterviolence, of oppression from the right and the left, of the rich getting richer and poor poorer, it is imperative for the church-in-mission to include the 'superior justice' of the Sermon on the Mount in its missionary agenda."

—David J. Bosch, *Transforming Mission* (Maryknoll: Orbis Books, 1993), p. 70.

Mission and peacemaking in the early church

How did the combination of mission and peacemaking play out in the early church? The conversion of Cornelius (Acts 10) gives some clues. It is striking that the *first* Gentile to become a follower of Jesus was a Roman centurion. Peter was sent by God to take the message of salvation to a Roman soldier of the same rank as those who crucified Jesus. This was peacemaking on a deeply personal and political level, with followers of Jesus building bridges to a representative of "the enemy."

With inspired words, Peter tells Cornelius that "God shows no partiality," and God himself was "preaching peace by Jesus Christ." Everyone who "believes in him receives forgiveness of sins through his name." While Peter spoke these words, the Holy Spirit "fell upon all who heard the word" (Acts 10:34-44). In the story of Cornelius we find the same powerful blend of factors that transformed the disciples meeting behind locked doors on resurrection Sunday: peace, forgiveness of sins, the Holy Spirit, and divine sending.

Paul—the greatest missionary of the early church—understood peacemaking to be at the heart of the good news. Few things better illustrated peacemaking than the end of hostility between Jews and Gentiles who came to know Jesus. Christ "is our peace," Paul said, and "in his flesh he has . . . broken down the dividing wall . . . between us" (Ephesians 2:14). In the first centuries of the Christian church, pagan writers commonly complained that Christians broke down the proper boundaries of society by freely mixing women and men, slave and free, rich and poor.

There must have been a lot of forgiveness exchanged for such a socially and economically diverse church to hold together. Women who suffered loss of power (or worse) in a male-dominated world must have extended forgiveness to men. Slaves must have forgiven masters who abused them. The poor must have forgiven those who once hoarded wealth.

For discussion

a. Do a word association with the term mission, and then with the word peace. List these on a flipchart or blackboard. Do the ideas or images that come to mind overlap or intersect? If so, how? If not, why not?

Church: Power to be reconcilers—How is God calling and sending?

When Jesus breathed the Holy Spirit on his followers, it was not to give them spiritual euphoria. In John's account, there was no dramatic expression such as tongues or prophecy. Instead, Jesus sent his Spirit-filled disciples on a mission of reconciliation: "If you forgive the sins of any, they are forgiven them; if you retain the sins of any, they are retained" (John 20:23).

When Peter took the good news of Jesus to the centurion Cornelius, Peter truly had to forgive. He could not retain the anger and bitterness that he and other disciples must have felt toward the Romans who killed Jesus. Peter himself—who denied and abandoned Jesus on the night of Jesus' arrest—had experienced profound forgiveness from his Lord. Jesus had brought Peter back into fellowship and even prepared a meal for Peter and the other disciples (John 21:9-14).

Because forgiveness and peacemaking are so closely tied to mission, we cannot be effective ambassadors for Christ unless we ourselves have been reconciled to God. Daily we come to God in worship for cleansing, healing, and forgiveness. We experience God's peace on a personal level as the Holy Spirit breathes into our lives. This inner peace gives us hope and strength to be agents of God's peacemaking in the world.

Church: The awesome task to forgive—How is God calling and sending?

The most awesome task Jesus gives the church is the power to forgive or to retain sins. This language in the fourth Gospel is similar to the teaching of Jesus in Matthew (18:18) that "whatever you bind on earth will be bound in heaven, and whatever you loose on earth will be loosed in heaven." What power the church has for being sent out into a hurting world! Jesus has given the *church* the power to extend forgiveness that registers eternally in heaven.

Picture how this may look in your congregation. Recovering alcoholics will be embraced as sisters and brothers. Inmates at the local prison will join in Bible study with members of the church. Men and women whose lives have been shattered by broken marriages will find healing and love among followers of Jesus. Those who have cheated on taxes, taken part in abortion, abused spouses, hoarded wealth, used pornography or enlisted in state-sponsored violence will confess their sin and start a new life. Such confession may not and should not always be public. But the church will provide confidential settings (with the pastor or in small groups) where individual members can speak openly about their lives and their need for God.

God's forgiveness will become tangible and visible in real human relationships in the church. Handshakes, embraces, and table fellowship will become familiar rituals of reconciliation. The circle of healing and hope will grow as the joy of restored community spills out beyond the walls of the church to attract neighbors and strangers.

Church: Responding in hope—How is God calling and sending?

Prairie Street Mennonite Church took no direct action in response to the murder on a nearby street, except for the time we prayed on location. Even that, though, was a significant action because it changed us. We got out of our pews and went to a place of deep need in our city.

It also reminded us of why a number of people in the congregation invest part or much of their lives in making the local community a place of hope. Jeannette teaches full time in an inner-city school. Many of the children come from poor or fractured homes.

Steve has worked over the last year to organize a program that brings local pastors together with schools and mental health agencies to support families in crisis. Several members of the congregation regularly volunteer as tutors at an elementary school where many children have parents who cannot or do not help them with homework. Maynard participates in a ministry to drug addicts and prostitutes on the city streets. Some members of the church have chosen to live in needy neighborhoods to be salt and light. Arlene has volunteered for years at a Christian-sponsored food pantry and job-training program for low-income adults. Some people of the congregation own businesses, work in medicine or other professional fields—and find ways to share the love of Jesus on the job.

For discussion

a. List the ways people in your congregation or group are involved in the local community (or elsewhere in the world) through work, volunteer roles, or mission. Thank God for these opportunities, and pray for each one.

b. What needs do you see for Christians to be peacemakers in the local community or in the wider world?

   Consider the possibility of every church member finding at least one direct involvement in peacemaking, mission, or service in the local community or elsewhere in the world. Probably only some members of your church will be able to participate full time in such activities. Everyone, though, can have at least some level of involvement in sharing the good news of Jesus.

c. Are you able to find ways to put words of invitation to your service and ministry? That is, do people with whom you work in your local or global mission know that you do so because of your commitment to Jesus Christ? Do you find ways to invite them to know and follow Jesus?

SESSION 3

One new humanity

Lois Barrett

IN A CHURCH in Minneapolis, immigrants from once-warring Ethiopia and Eritrea worship in the same pew. In Markham, Illinois, a congregation intentionally includes black and white members. In a church in Kansas, an ex-con and his young daughter become practically family members of a middle-class couple.

But just crossing boundaries of politics, race, and class is not enough. People like the couple in the following story are struggling to find community and identity:

He was American agnostic; she was Danish Catholic. They met in Denmark, where he became a Catholic to please her parents. They decided to travel around the world together. Somewhere in northern Africa, they decided to get married. The only person available to perform the wedding ceremony was a Muslim imam—so the couple became Muslim. When they were in Israel, they became strict Hasidic Jews. Later, they became secular Jews. At last report, they had no community. They were like the "strangers and aliens" in Ephesians 2:19. They were "not a people" (1 Peter 2:10).

Biblical texts

Ephesians 2:11-22

[11] So then, remember that at one time you Gentiles by birth, called "the uncircumcision" by those who are called "the circumcision"—a physical circumcision made in the flesh by human hands— [12] remember that you

were at that time without Christ, being aliens from the commonwealth of Israel, and strangers to the covenants of promise, having no hope and without God in the world. [13] But now in Christ Jesus you who once were far off have been brought near by the blood of Christ. [14] For he is our peace; in his flesh he has made both groups into one and has broken down the dividing wall, that is the hostility between us. [15] He has abolished the law with its commandments and ordinances, that he might create in himself one new humanity in place of two, thus making peace, [16] and might reconcile both groups to God in one body through the cross, thus putting to death that hostility through it. [17] So he came and proclaimed peace to you who were far off and peace to those who were near; [18] for through him both of us have access in one Spirit to the Father. [19] So then you are no longer strangers and aliens, but you are citizens with the saints and also members of the household of God, [20] built upon the foundation of the apostles and prophets, with Christ Jesus himself as the cornerstone. [21] In him the whole structure is joined together and grows into a holy temple in the Lord; [22] in whom you also are built together spiritually into a dwelling place for God.

1 Peter 2:9-10

[9] But you are a chosen race, a royal priesthood, a holy nation, God's own people, in order that you may proclaim the mighty acts of him who called you out of darkness into his marvelous light.
[10] Once you were not a people, but now you are God's people; once you had not received mercy, but now you have received mercy.

Context—Where are we?

In Ephesians 2 (and in most of the New Testament) the biggest dividing wall in the church was between Jew and Gentile, "the circumcision" versus "the uncircumcision." Circumcision was a symbol of the division of Jew and Gentile. It was a symbol of Jewish peoplehood. Gentiles were the "the nations" *(ethnoi)*, the "ethnics." To be a people, an *ethnos* ("nation"), went beyond geographical boundaries. In fact, in the first century of the Christian era, more Jews were living in the Dispersion than in Judea, Samaria, and Galilee. To be a Jew was an identity issue.

Ephesians 2 recognizes that the "dividing wall" between Jew and Gentile has represented real hostility. In fact, this hostility is mentioned twice—in verses 14 and 16. For Jews, the world was divided into two groups: the "circumcision" and the "uncircumcision," the Jews and the non-Jews.

Many of the words found in Ephesians 2 have political meaning. It calls Gentiles "aliens [foreigners] from the commonwealth [*politeías*, from which we get the word politics] of Israel." They are "strangers to the covenant of promise," the covenant that was the foundation of Jewish faith and national identity. First Peter 2:9-10 also uses political language: "Once you were not a people, but now you are God's people." You are "a holy nation *[ethnos]*, God's own people."

The ancient world had many ethnic and national divisions. Some were based on class, especially slave and free, Roman citizens and noncitizens. There were divisions between men and women, barbarian and civilized, rich and poor, literate and illiterate. These divisions were often the flashpoint for hostility between groups—hostility ranging from fear of strangers to genocide.

The human condition is that we want to separate ourselves from people who are different from us; we want the people around us to be just like us. For children, wanting to be just like the people close to us is good; that is the way children are socialized and gain identity as part of a group. But this good desire can be corrupted and turned into racial or ethnic discrimination or even ethnic cleansing when, as we grow up, we expect everybody around us to be just like us—or want to eliminate them if they are not just like us. Our world today is full of ethnic, racial, and national divisions that bring about hostility.

For discussion

a. Where do people in our society get their identity?
b. What are the dividing walls that keep people apart?
c. What are the powers and systems that keep groups of people hostile to each other?
d. What are the consequences of holding these various identities too tightly?

While some people in our postmodern world are hanging onto various racial, ethnic, national, and class identities, others seem to be drifting without direction, without identity, without a stable face-to-face community. They are disconnected, or they move quickly from one connection to another. They are "not a people." They are "strangers to the covenants of promise, having no hope and without God in the world." They are like the wandering couple of the story found at the beginning of this session.

For discussion

a. Do you know people who don't seem to have any community, who are "aliens" (outsiders) and "strangers" everywhere? How do they act? What do they say?
b. Write on a piece of paper three nouns to describe yourself that say something about your identity—Who am I? Then share with the group.

Good news—What is God doing?

In the midst of all these competing identities and ethnicities, God through Christ is in mission. Ephesians 2 uses five phrases to describe what God in Christ Jesus is doing.

Christ brings people near. People who were far away are "brought near" to God and to the "covenants of promise." Through Christ both Jews and Gentiles "have access in one Spirit to the Father." At the price of death on a cross, Christ is bringing people into relationship with God and into relationship with each other. It is not that each group has its own separate access to God, but the access is "in one Spirit." When people are drawn nearer to God, they are drawn nearer to each other. Through Christ, God is bringing together people who are different from each other, and who may not have even liked each other.

This bringing together of people who are not alike is key to God's purposes in the world. In fact, every atom in the universe is witness to this purpose. Even the smallest blade of grass by the roadside is made up of atoms that, within them, hold positive and negative charges together. This is what God intends for all of creation—holding opposites together, bringing people closer together who, because of sin, are tempted to be far apart.

Christ creates in himself one new humanity. In Christ, people are not only brought near; they become a new people—"a new humanity" or a "new human being." Ephesians 2 emphasizes this: "He has made both groups into one" (v. 14), "that he might create in himself one new humanity in place of two" (v. 15), "and might reconcile both groups to God in one body" (v. 16). God's creative work did not end on the seventh day of creation. God is creating the church as a people of God, in continuity with the "commonwealth of Israel" (v. 12), but made new in Christ. It is in Christ, in fact, that this new social reality includes both Jews and Gentiles. First Peter refers to this creation of a people thus: "Once you were not a people; now you are God's people." Something new has come into being because God has created it.

Christ breaks down hostility. "The one new humanity" is made possible by Christ's action of breaking down the dividing wall, or hostility, between Jewish Christians and Gentile Christians. The law that served to separate Jew and Gentile no longer does so. In fact, the whole church is now the "chosen race," and the words used to describe the people of Israel in Exodus 19:5-6 are applied to the church—Jew and Gentile—in 1 Peter 2:9. Instead of violence, slander, or other forms of hostility, there is peace.

Christ reconciles. In Ephesians 2, this reconciliation of both groups to God happens together, "in one body." Right relationships with God and right relationships with people are intimately connected. However, this reconciliation takes place at a price—

Jesus' death on the cross. The one body, the church, is reconciled through faith in Jesus and faithfulness to the way of Jesus, a way that led to the cross. In relationship with its crucified Lord, the church experiences that the previous hostility is "put to death." God's mission in Christ is reconciling the world (see 2 Corinthians 5:18-19).

Christ is our peace, makes peace, and proclaims peace. Here, peace is certainly the absence of hostility. But more than that, peace involves reconciliation and right relationships. First of all in Ephesians 2, Christ *is* our peace. The peace among once-hostile groups comes about "in Christ Jesus" (v. 13), "in his flesh" (v. 14). Both groups being in the body of Christ means peace. Second, Christ *makes* peace. Through God's action in Christ, Christ does the work of peacemaking and reconciliation. Third, Christ *proclaims* peace, speaks the word of peace to "you who were far off" and "those who were near." Peace involves being, doing, and speaking.

For discussion

a. What is good news in this text?
b. What have you perceived God to be doing?
- to bring people near?
- to create one new humanity?
- to break down dividing walls of hostility?
- to reconcile?
- to make and proclaim peace?

c. How is Ephesians 2 calling us to repent or change?

Church—How is God calling and sending us?

In the Roman world of the first century, there were three social arenas: the city, the household, and the temple. The city (*polis*, from which we get the word "political") was the group of citizens who gathered for decision making. The New Testament word that we translate "church" is *ecclesia*, a secular Greek word meaning "town meeting" or "political assembly." The household (*oikonomia*, from which we get the word "economy") included parents, children, grandparents, and others who were related by blood. It also included slaves or others involved in the family business. The household was an economic unit as well as a familial unit. The temple was a place of religious ritual, whether the Jewish temple in Jerusalem or pagan temples elsewhere in the Mediterranean world. Sometimes the temple was seen as a residence of the god to which it was dedicated.

"Why is it that so many sectors of the historically Christian parts of the world and other areas experiencing rapid church growth still are caught so deeply in the grip of unrestrained materialism and increasing concentration of wealth in the hands of a few? Why are crushing burdens of oppression on those who are weak and powerless tolerated and even ignored? Why are moral values and public behavior, even in areas with substantial Christian presence, deteriorating to depths not even seen in Sodom and Gomorrah? Surely these are not the fruits that are expected from those who are Jesus' disciples."

—Engel and Dyrness, *Changing the Mind of Missions* (Downers Grove, Ill: InterVarsity Press) p. 56.

Ephesians 2:19-22 uses all three social arenas to describe the church, the people of God. (1) Christians are "citizens with the saints." First Peter 2:9 calls the church a "holy nation," a "*royal* priesthood." There is a political character to the church. (2) Christians are "members of the household of God." There is a family character to the church as well as an economic character. And (3) Christians are seen as a "holy temple in the Lord," "a dwelling place for God," a structure held together by Christ (Ephesians 2:21). As a body, they are a "royal *priesthood*" (1 Peter 2:9).

In all these social arenas, the church is to make a public witness to the reign of God. The church demonstrates a new allegiance to God, different from allegiances to the city or to the Roman Empire. What was important was citizenship in the reign of God, whether or not one was a Roman citizen. The early church proclaimed, "Jesus is Lord," while others said, "Caesar is Lord." Others could look at the church and see the "holy nation."

The church demonstrates a new kind of household, where there is no longer Jew or Greek, slave or free, male or female. New relationships of "brother" and "sister" in the church would have been a clear alternative to the social class and ethnic divisions of the Roman world. Others could look at the church and see the "household of God."

The church demonstrates a new kind of temple, not built of stone and marble, but of people. Together, the church is built into a dwelling place for God in the Spirit. Its cornerstone is Christ Jesus. Its foundation is the apostles and prophets. The Spirit of God is in the midst of the church wherever it gathers, wherever it witnesses.

For discussion

a. In our society, many people have different ideas of what the church is. Some think the church is to be a chaplain to society, marrying, burying, and praying at public events. Others think of the church as a voluntary association, a kind of religious club or organization. That is, in fact, the legal status of the church in Canada and the United States. Still others see the church as a vendor of religious goods and services, provided to "meet the needs" of its own members and those outside the church.

   If a congregation is operating out of one of these popular understandings of the church, what changes would it need to make to become:
   - a holy nation?
   - the household of God?
   - a holy temple in the Lord?

b. Does identity as the people of God wipe out all other identities?

c. What characteristics make a people a "Christian nation"?

d. How do these texts call and send the church to participate in God's mission in the world?

SESSION 4

Taking risks in the power of the Holy Spirit

Gilberto Flores

A congregation faces a dilemma

"What shall we do? Carnival is coming to the gates of the church!"

In 1976, the Center of Christian Discipleship Mennonite Church in San Pedro Sula, Honduras, was confronted with the news that the city committee in charge of carnival had decided to celebrate it that year in the street in front of their church building. There would be two nights with much music and dancing in the public street, an activity that would interfere with one of the important meetings of the congregation. The church council proposed three alternatives: (1) close that night and all stay home, (2) have a meeting of only thirty minutes, or (3) shift that night to meetings of the groups that met in homes. They wanted to avoid the din, disorder, and debauchery that normally come with carnival. The church council did not want to have decent families exposed to the embarrassment of merrymakers carousing in front of the church building. The council left the meeting believing that, at least for this event, for this group of brothers and sisters, it was better to separate themselves from the world that could contaminate them.

On the following Sunday the council's concern was laid before the whole congregation. The council hoped for strong support for the idea of canceling the meeting scheduled for that date. There were many questions, and to the surprise of the council, the congregation decided to create a committee to develop proactive responses to carnival. Two weeks later a survey of the 150-member congregation was completed. Finally, at the next congregational meeting, there was unanimous agreement "that, under the leadership of the pastor, the church board would prepare a two-day program that would give witness to Jesus Christ in the midst of the disorderliness of carnival."

A program was then prepared for an event to be held in the parking lot. It included special music presented by their talented youth group, as well as coffee and refreshments for those who came in. Literature about the Mennonite Church was provided. Chairs were available so that people could rest while listening to the music or for conversation with more than fifty volunteers from the church who would testify about Jesus during the evenings.

A women's group from the church prayed for two weeks, asking for God's help. This group continued in prayer during the whole first night of carnival. At the beginning of carnival, the sisters and brothers were timid and fearful. To conquer their fear, everyone united in a time of prayer. After praying, things changed. Some church members mingled with the dancers and invited them to come in to rest and listen to "our kind of music."

Various things happened during these evenings. A group of carnival organizers asked the church to reduce the length of its concerts so that the people would go out and dance in the street. But the people preferred to be in the parking lot, where the church had arranged for several musical presentations. Criticism also came from leaders of other Christian groups, who suggested that it was improper for the church to jeopardize its testimony.

By the end of carnival, the brothers and sisters had shared their faith with more than 500 people. Fifty of them decided to begin a relationship with God. As for the church, there grew a sense of urgency to share the gospel and to witness to the reign of God. A short time later the congregation began to organize congregations in different locations in the city. By 1985, five new Mennonite congregations were flourishing in San Pedro Sula. One of the church members who participated actively in the whole project summarized their experience by saying, "The devil brought evil to our doors, but God gave us the Holy Spirit to overcome our fears and overcome evil. To God be the glory!"

Biblical texts

Luke 23:44-46

> [44] It was now about noon, and darkness came over the whole land until three in the afternoon, [45] while the sun's light failed; and the curtain of the temple was torn in two. [46] Then Jesus, crying with a loud voice, said, "Father, into your hands I commend my spirit." Having said this, he breathed his last.

Acts 4:23-33

> [23] After they were released, they [Peter and John] went to their friends and reported what the chief priests and the elders had said to them. [24] When they heard it, they raised their voices together to God and said, "Sovereign Lord, who made the heaven and the earth, the sea, and everything in them, [25] it is you who said by the Holy Spirit through our ancestor David, your servant:
>
> 'Why did the Gentiles rage,
> and the peoples imagine vain things?
> [26] The kings of the earth took their stand,
> and the rulers have gathered together
> against the Lord and against his Messiah.'
>
> [27] For in this city, in fact, both Herod and Pontius Pilate, with the Gentiles and the peoples of Israel, gathered together against your holy servant Jesus, whom you anointed, [28] to do whatever your hand and your plan had predestined to take place [29] And now, Lord, look at their threats, and grant to your servants to speak your word with all boldness, [30] while you stretch out your hand to heal, and signs and wonders are performed through the name of your holy servant Jesus." [31] When

> they had prayed, the place in which they were gathered together was shaken; and they were all filled with the Holy Spirit and spoke the word of God with boldness. [32] Now the whole group of those who believed were of one heart and soul, and no one claimed private ownership of any possessions, but everything they owned was held in common. [33] With great power the apostles gave their testimony to the resurrection of the Lord, Jesus, and great grace was upon them all.

Context—Where are we?

For the Gospel of Luke, the central theme is the work and the person of Jesus. It has the character of instruction, of thoughtful and reflective testimony about the events and the teachings of Jesus. For this reason the Luke 23:44-46 narrative seems to reflect the liturgy of the community of faith. Apparently, Luke writes to interpret and not just to narrate the events at Calvary. These events, like scenes of a drama, invite readers to think, motivate them to consider, and challenge them to commit themselves to this drama. Luke employs such visual images as the darkness, the veil of the temple torn in two, the cry and the surrender of the Son of God, and the silent moment of death to help them understand.

These descriptions are invitations to enter the mystery of the love of God as demonstrated in the incarnation of Jesus. This mystery reveals the good news as loving, serving, walking with the poor, bringing hope in affliction, proclaiming the truth of the reign of God, making accessible to all humanity the message of reconciliation, and sharing risks that can lead to loneliness, abandonment, and eventually death. Luke shows us Jesus as one who was obedient to the Father and submissive in carrying out the mission that has been entrusted to him.

In the Acts of the Apostles, the church appeals to the lordship of Jesus Christ in defining its loyalty and its relationship with the society and the world. Each time the community of faith is confronted with a difficult circumstance, it understands this experience in the light of the person and the acts of Jesus. In the same way, a sign shows the continuation of the purposes of God manifested in Jesus Christ. The victory over evil and sin is a witness that the Lord is alive. Repentance of sins is possible because the love of Christ flows through the Holy Spirit to the community of faith. Persecutions are expressions of evil that come against the brothers and sisters just as it did against their Master. Persecution, prison, and violence against the church are not the exception, but the rule. These are expected for followers of the risen Lord.

The Churches, like Jesus, intentionally accept the risks inherent in carrying out the mission. They know that, if they want to be faithful to the calling that they have received, they must break out of their isolation and search for the people of their surrounding areas, so that they can be instruments of blessing. They also accept the fact that they will be objects of rejection and intended evil. These are described in four scenes in Acts 4:

A sign of the Holy Spirit was shown through the healing of a lame man, followed by a sermon that challenges the hearers to make a commitment to Jesus Christ.

An encounter with the structures of power. Those who exercise power are indignant at the boldness of the disciples in proclaiming the good news. The established religion and the political powers, working in concert, take the disciples before the authorities. The disciples are ordered to stop preaching about the resurrected Jesus and are threatened in order to intimidate them. The brothers demonstrate their new Christian identity and courageously affirm their faithfulness to the resurrected Christ. They confess their intention to obey only the one who has called them and sent them to carry out the mission commended to them.

The disciples pray. In this prayer we can identify two themes: (1) a confession of faith through words that exalt their Lord and Savior. And (2) they recognize the divine plan and ask God for wisdom. When the disciples pray, they request help as well as demand power and confidence to continue to speak the good news. They ask that signs of the presence of the Holy Spirit accompany the word. The disciples do not ask to be free of persecution, but for help not to be dismayed by the enemy's pursuit of them. God shows them his presence and, as a consequence, they all are filled with the Holy Spirit and speak the word of God with boldness.

The community of faith takes on a lifestyle that reflects its intention to be a community of equality, solidarity, and generosity, a community that shocks people because of the form of its obedience to its Master. Little by little, the church becomes a demonstration of justice in the midst of a corrupt world.

For discussion

a. Can you imagine a group of people living this lifestyle without affecting those around them?
b. Was there something different about Jesus and his disciples in the minds of the common people that made them an object of acceptance or rejection? What was it?
c. Were the actions of Jesus and his disciples neutral in the context of his time? Why or why not?

Calling and sending—What is God doing?

In the two passages we have read there seems to be no reference to the Great Commission, to making disciples, or to the assignment of a mission field. Instead, Luke refers to the death of Jesus. It is an invitation to enter into the mystery of the love of God (John 3:16). This is a love that invites us to draw near to God and moves us to act like God. Our God, who loves so much, cannot remain unmoved before human need. God in Christ, within history, enters the world as a missionary. Jesus, crucified and later resurrected, is sufficient proof that God is in mission.

The disciples understand that the Lord counts on them to continue this mission. That is what the disciples demonstrated for us in Acts 4. The rejection of Jesus by the religious leaders and their association with political power in order to achieve the death of Jesus are seen by the disciples as a trap of evil to oppose God's plan to save the world (vv. 26-27). But God, who will use it to bring about his great missionary project, knows that trap. The disciples say it this way: "to do whatever your hand and your plan had determined ahead of time to take place." They see themselves as continuing God's strategy shown through Jesus Christ. For this reason the disciples do not tremble before threats; in contrast they say, "We will obey God rather than you." They consider themselves as sent and know themselves as faithful. They see themselves invited to walk a new path, and they accept their vocation. The disciples believe they are called, and identify with their Savior. They pray to be worthy to proclaim the reign of God. "Lord," they say, "grant to your servants to speak your word with all boldness."

The risk taking of Jesus and his disciples—What is God doing?

Can we say that we will go forward seeking, just as Jesus and his disciples, to be considered voluntary candidates for death and suffering? The threat of suffering and the possibility of death for the followers of Jesus are a defensive reaction of evil to the life-giving power of the gospel. Certainly, without the power of the Holy Spirit, it is difficult to face these external risks. With the help of the Holy Spirit we can be faithful and obedient.

While the possibility of suffering or death is not to be sought, the risk is to be accepted. Jesus prays in Gethsemane, "Father, if you are willing, remove this cup from me; yet, not my will but yours be done" (Luke 22:42). The disciples pray, saying, "Look at their threats, and grant to your servants to speak your word with all boldness" (Acts 4:29). Both prayers express an interest in doing the will of God; they also express an insecurity that causes the heart to pound.

Jesus completed the tasks that his Father commended to him. He lived on the boundaries that separate the marginalized from the privileged and dominant. Jesus assumed that his task was the evangelization of the people in those communities of marginality and weakness. His mission and the way that he chose to carry it out are a scandal. His teaching turned society's accepted values upside down. Jesus' taking on the human manifestations of love,

Enabled by the giving of the Holy Spirit at Pentecost, missions is the extension of the mighty work that Christ embodied as he restored God's reign on the earth—atoning for human sin on the cross and conquering sin and death in the resurrection. And it is an anticipation of what God one-day will do when Christ returns in glory to renew the earth. It is God-originated, Christ-centered and Spirit-empowered.

—James F. Engel and William A. Dyrness, *Changing the Mind of Missions* (Downers Grove, Ill.: InterVarsity Press, 2000), p. 37.

acceptance, respect, hope, and right relationship offends an exclusive society. Death was its consequence.

The disciples would confront the same thing. If they wanted to be like their Master, they had to go to the same school. When the disciples decided to use the keys to the kingdom and to be a sign of the presence of God, the leaders of the temple and religion, who had delivered Jesus to death, saw in them the continuation of a danger that they wanted to eliminate quickly.

Taking risks in the power of the Holy Spirit—Jesus and his disciples—What is God doing?

The disciples' risk was to go out into the street and witness to the resurrected Jesus, and to demonstrate by signs the presence of the reign of God. Their risk was to offer to sinners an entrance into the celebration of the kingdom promised by Jesus Christ.

It was dangerous to organize themselves as a community of faith alternative to the system, a community that served as a place or human space where all men, women, and children could have the same level of relationship, treatment, and consideration (Acts 4). It was an even greater risk to open a way that would develop relationships among different cultures, for example, the Hellenist group and the Hebrew group (Acts 6).

For Jesus it was dangerous to establish a different treatment of women, using respect, an attitude that promoted dialogue. He was with the marginalized, the poor, and the sick. Jesus' prophetic voice regarding social sin stirred up the structures of power, religious and political. When he traveled among the towns and villages announcing the reign of God, it was enough to believe and repent; thus giving people who had no hope the opportunity to enjoy the signs of God's grace. This and all the other things Jesus did were risks.

The disciples succeeded in establishing themselves as the church in Jerusalem and began to enjoy the advantages of having grown in numbers. Then the Holy Spirit reminded them that a church without mission is not a church. The Spirit pushed them outside so that they would walk in mission and accept the risks of their pilgrimage. And when they believed that Judaism and Christian faith were a secure formula, a comfort zone, God called other men and women, like Paul, to show that the last frontier for witness had not yet been reached.

Although this way involved risks, neither Jesus nor his disciples walked alone. The Holy Spirit stood with them to guide, teach, strengthen, and protect them. They received power to carry out the mission and opened doors for them where they wanted to go. Later on, the early church enjoyed this same care and blessing from the Holy Spirit. And this is still true today in the life of the church of Jesus Christ.

Taking risks in the power of the Holy Spirit—the church today—How is God calling and sending?

The Christian faith today is not a religion separate from society. Except in countries where the dominant religion is not Christian, most people know something about the Christian faith. Ours is a society where Christianity is accepted in many places. No one will suffer injury for practicing his or her faith. So how are we to speak of risks?

Risk can begin inside the church. For example, it can be risky to accept changes in the way of doing things, or if one is disposed, to listen to the voice of God calling to the church to be responsible in fulfilling God's mission. There is risk in leaving a comfort zone that arises from the tradition of the church and its history. There is risk in opening oneself to other cultures when the congregation is part of the majority culture.

Yet, risk is the nature of the church, its calling or vocation, and the location where God has placed it to be faithful. There are also many risks and many blessings when the church sees itself as a holistic community, with a holistic gospel, with a holistic mission. That church understands that its boldness is not located in its own existence, but in the purpose that God has in giving it life through the Holy Spirit.

The church can be holistic when it understands itself as an evangelizing community. This is not to say it is a community that practices "evangelistic" proselytism. An evangelizing community is one whose actions within its community correspond with its actions beyond the community. To be evangelistic is to proclaim Jesus Christ and his reign and to show forth the signs of the presence of the Holy Spirit. It also means to bring together those who believe as a group of those renewed as the new humanity of the reign of God. Such a community engages in:

proclaiming by word and deed the gospel of the reign of God.
teaching the word to believers so that they can give witness and present a defense of their faith.
worship that offers to God the sacrifices of gratitude and praise.
service, an expression of open arms to help those in need.
discipleship, a lifelong process that allows the Christian to live responsibly, equipped to carry out the mission.
reconciliation, making and bringing about peace.
restoration, not only of the human person, but of creation as well.

One person cannot carry out this challenging task alone. Evangelism is the duty for the whole believing community. This community opens itself to ongoing dialogue with the surrounding society, shares the contents of the faith, knows how to practice it, understands how to listen to those outside the church, and is able to read the signs of the times. It is a community of faith that cares about fulfilling the command of Jesus: Go from across the street to around the world and make disciples!

For discussion

a. Can we speak about the risks today for the church in the same way that we read about them in the book of Acts? Describe them.
b. Which risks can appear on the horizon of the church when it gives witness?
c. Should the church intentionally take risks? Why or why not?
d. What should be the shape of the "evangelizing community," the church that proclaims the *evangel*, the good news, by its witness and by its life together?

SESSION 5

Missional practices: Making disciples of all nations

James Krabill

IN LATE 1913, William Wade Harris, a fifty-three-year-old West African prophet-evangelist, left his native Liberia and stepped across the French colonial boundary into neighboring Ivory Coast, equipped with little more than a passionate desire to share the good news of Jesus. Walking barefoot from village to village along the coast, Harris challenged people everywhere to lay aside their traditional objects of worship and turn instead to the one, true God.

Harris' ministry lasted a mere eighteen months. But during that time, an estimated 100,000 to 200,000 people from over a dozen different ethnic groups accepted the evangelist's call, received baptism, and took their first steps toward a new life in Christ.

How much these early believers really understood about Christian faith is hard to know. But Harris did what he could to ensure a sound beginning by teaching them the Ten Commandments, the Apostles' Creed, and the Lord's Prayer. Additional advice he offered included counsel on husband-wife relationships, intertribal conflict, Christlike attitudes toward the oppressive French colonial government, ideas for worship, and suggestions on how to select the preachers and twelve apostles who would give spiritual leadership to the scores of newly emerging faith communities.

Preaching, baptizing, teaching, making disciples. One might wonder whether Harris had heard of the last will and testament left by Jesus to his own disciples as recorded for us in Matthew 28:16-20. Well, yes, of course, he had!

For discussion

a. What reactions do you have to the William Wade Harris story? If an evangelist can't stay around to do follow-up and there is no local church or mission structure to fall back on, is it better not to evangelize at all?

Biblical texts

Matthew 28:16-20

[16] Now the eleven disciples went to Galilee, to the mountain to which Jesus had directed them. [17] When they saw him, they worshiped him; but some doubted. [18] And Jesus came and said to them, "All authority in heaven and on earth has been given to me. [19] Go therefore and make disciples of all nations, baptizing them in the name of the Father and of the Son and of the Holy Spirit, [20] and teaching them to obey everything that I have commanded you. And remember, I am with you always, to the end of the age."

Ephesians 3:8-10

[8] Although I am the very least of all the saints, this grace was given to me to bring to the Gentiles the news of the boundless riches of Christ, [9] and to make everyone see what is the plan of the mystery hidden for ages in God who created all things; so that through the church the wisdom of God in its rich variety might now be made known to the rulers and authorities in the heavenly places.

Context—Where are we?

The whole thing must have felt pretty overwhelming to the eleven disciples assembled in Galilee for their final farewell gathering with Jesus. It was not exactly the mountaintop experience they had anticipated. They had come wanting to worship. Yet, according to Matthew, even in these final moments with Jesus, "some doubted" (28:17).

Doubting had come rather easy for the disciples in recent weeks. Judas Iscariot, as we know, had doubted himself right out of the group. And Thomas had nearly followed suit. Peter had every reason to doubt whether he could ever regain the trust of his colleagues after his dismal midnight performance in the high priest's courtyard and subsequent gentle reprimand from the Lord: "Simon, do you love me? Do you love me? DO YOU LOVE ME?" How embarrassing is it to hear *that* question repeated three times by Jesus in front of the entire disciple band?

It was, of course, reassuring for everyone—yet rather confusing and almost unbelievable—to see Jesus back from the dead. Just when they had gotten used to Jesus being gone, there he was again! Well, *some* of the time. It was sort of an in-and-out experience. Definitely different from the ministry years when being with Jesus was an everyday, all-day affair.

Questions only multiplied as the new reality began to sink in. So Jesus really was . . . *is* the Messiah? Is that what we're to conclude from the events of the past few weeks? If that's true, why doesn't he drop in more frequently so we can ask him about the meaning of all this for our new life together? And what's he saying just now about teaching all nations? Let's start by assuming that can't possibly mean the Samaritans, the Phoenicians, the Rom . . . *no*, let's not even entertain *that* thought!

"Make disciples?" Yeah, right! Given our track record, we'll be *great* at that! Most of us were hiding behind the bushes watching Jesus die just a few short weeks ago. He can't be serious about *that* proposal. *I* would never entrust this fickle bunch with such an assignment. And I can't imagine *he* would either!

What I find most intriguing about the questions and doubts of these early believers is their striking similarity to many of those felt and voiced by people, including Christians, even today.

• ***Is Jesus really the Messiah?*** A good guy? Certainly! A remarkable teacher? No doubt! But beyond that, what is so special about Jesus? There are, after all, lots of other great people out there—Buddha, Mohammed, and Gandhi . . . to name only a few.

• ***Are we really supposed to baptize all nations?*** Isn't that just a bit arrogant on our part? What gives us the right to impose our views on people of other faiths? Don't all spiritual paths lead up the mountain to the same God anyway?

• ***How sound a strategy is it to have disciples making other disciples?*** Most of the Christians I know have so much pain and brokenness in their own lives they would be of little help in nurturing others to a more mature faith. In any case, don't expect much from me in this department. Definitely not my gift! I am a timid personality-type. I've never attended Bible college or seminary to get training in this area. My new job doesn't allow me any extra time for this type of activity. And furthermore, aren't we paying the pastor to do this work on our behalf?

Gospel—What is God doing?

When we have finally reached the end of the road with all of the questions and excuses our small minds can muster, Jesus comes to us. As he did to that first band of disciples Jesus calls into question our limited cultural understandings and assumptions. He invites us to reconsider the radical nature of his claim on our lives:

You've been wondering what's so special about me? Well, actually, all authority in heaven and on earth has been given to me. That's pretty special, wouldn't you say?

Have you stopped to ponder the implications of what that means? This project God has assigned to me is of cosmic proportions. Oh, sure, it includes you and your tribe. But don't think so small. Think universe! Think all creatures, all nations, all spiritual powers in high and low places. That should keep your mind occupied for a while.

And speaking of occupied, I need your assistance in spreading the word. If God's project is where all of history is going, then all people everywhere have the right to know about it.

You want more details about the project? Why don't you start by putting into practice and passing along to others what I've already taught you. Not just *some* of it. *All* of it! Tell the whole story, everything I said, every person I healed, every prayer I uttered, every injustice I denounced, every broken spirit I made whole, every demon I cast out, every sin I have forgiven.

Tell it all! And when people express a desire to be a part of this new thing God is doing and organize their lives around the values and priorities of that reality, celebrate their commitment by baptizing them into the family of faith.

Starting to sound a bit overwhelming? It is. In fact, it's way beyond you. Reason why I pledge to you my presence and power until . . . well, let's just make that until "the end of the age"—unless you can think of some reason you might prefer a shorter-term policy.

For discussion

a. Read the biblical texts for this session and share any new thoughts from this reading.
b. Compare briefly the Matthew text with other Great Commission passages found in the New Testament (see Mark 16:12-18; John 20:19-21; and Acts 1:6-11).

Church—How is God calling and sending?

It was really not until after Pentecost that the early church got the power and got the point. And then, suddenly, nothing apparently could stop them from being about the ongoing work of Jesus. Of the various "Great Commissions" found in the New Testament (Mark 16:15; John 20:21; Acts 1:8; etc.), it is Matthew's version that insists the most on mission as *disciple making*—on baptizing and on teaching all that Jesus had commanded.

The disciples were not particularly well suited for carrying out this assignment. Most of them, like ninety-five percent of their compatriots in first-century Palestine, were likely illiterate with little or no formal education (Acts 4:13). Yet, empowered by the

Holy Spirit, they went about their task with great zeal in the synagogue, before learned councils, in conversations with Roman officials, and wherever else they could get an audience.

Their model and mandate, of course, came from Jesus—the teacher. Although lacking accreditation as a disciple of any of the established rabbinical schools, Jesus was often given this title by his listeners because he spoke with more authority than those who had properly earned their titles in more traditional ways.

Matthew's Gospel provides us with five substantial blocks of Jesus' teaching. (Could this have been done intentionally to present Jesus as the new Moses with a parallel being drawn to the five books of the Law? Some think so.) In any case, Jesus begins his ministry here by calling out the disciples for the purpose of mission (4:19), and then providing them with sound instruction about:

- kingdom living (chapters 5-7, the Sermon on the Mount);
- kingdom mission (chapter 10);
- parables on how to recognize the kingdom (chapter 13);
- healthy relationships within the kingdom (chapter 18);
- warnings about what to expect before the last days of the kingdom (chapters 23-25).

The ministry of Jesus, as presented by Matthew, so beautifully models what the Great Commission in chapter 28 actually calls for "making disciples" and "teaching them" the essentials for living under God's reign.

To what was Jesus actually referring when he advised his disciples to teach obedience to *everything* he had commanded them"? Some believe "everything" may have been the five discourses described above. Others think it refers to the summary version of Jesus' teaching as found in the Sermon on the Mount. Any or all of these would, of course, be a marvelous introduction to what life looks like when it is centered on kingdom values. For this reason, the book of Matthew was the church's most popular Gospel during the second century of the Christian era. They needed teaching materials for the growing number of converts entering the church in search of greater clarity on how to live as a follower of Jesus.

The church has not always done the best job of holding its teaching ministries and evangelistic functions together, even though the words of Jesus in Matthew 28 will not permit us to do otherwise. "*Through the church*," writes the apostle Paul to the believers in Ephesus, "the wisdom of God in its rich variety [is] made known" (3:10).

If, however, the church turns inward and becomes self-absorbed in its teaching functions, structures and preoccupations, then God's wisdom never escapes the confines of God's people to penetrate the hearts and lives of those beyond the faith community. At times in the history of the church this has, in fact, been the case.

Our first Gospel is essentially a missionary text. It was primarily because of his missionary vision that Matthew set out to write his Gospel, not to compose a life of Jesus but to provide guidance to a community in crisis on how it should understand its calling and mission.

—David J. Bosch, *Transforming Mission* (Maryknoll: Orbis Books, 1993), p. 57.

In some church communities, for example, Sunday schools were first initiated as a means of attracting and connecting with the specific neighborhood in which a given congregation happened to find itself. With time, however, the educational interests and needs of the congregation's own children began to take precedence over any other considerations, until finally it became evident that the original vision for the Sunday school had been lost altogether. In some instances, summer Bible school programs were then introduced as attempts to rekindle the earlier fire for local mission, but many of these, too, underwent transformation when the congregation became its own best client and neighborhood connections gradually dried up and faded away.

In contrast to this is the situation where evangelism has taken precedence over teaching, where primary attention is given to increasing the number of converts with little consideration as to how these believers will become true disciples of Christ, knowledgeable of and obedient to "everything that [he has] commanded." In such instances, Christian faith and understanding remain little more than a veneer, failing to penetrate in any significant way the outward surface of a person's life.

Some observers of religious trends would suggest that this is precisely what is happening for much of the church in North America. Biblical literacy is declining and less attention is given to the inroads of consumerism, pop culture, and general moral decadence in the lives of many Christians. As a result some have begun to refer to the religious reality in our society as "cosmetic Christianity"—a superficial version of faith flowing like a river through the continent "two miles wide, but only two inches deep."

The same might be said, but for different reasons, about the challenges the church is facing in other parts of the world. Many have spoken about the statistics: In 1900, there were only ten million Christians in all of Africa; by 2000 that number had grown to 360 million. In 1900 only 9.2 percent of Africans were Christian; in 2000, 45.9 percent of the population claimed Christian faith. Today, as Mennonite mission worker David A. Shank has noted, "Africa holds, without rival, the distinction of being the place where the largest number of people have moved into the Christian stream of history in the shortest amount of time."

We all rejoice in what God to doing in Africa. It serves as a great source of inspiration for Western Christians, and it will change the face of world Christianity forever. At the same time, the challenges confronting this new family of faith are enormous as they look to the future. As one African observer put it recently: "The church in Africa is like an elephant tottering precariously on chicken legs. The elephant is the rapidly growing church itself, with thousands of new converts joining the ranks each day. The chicken legs are the insufficient educational structures currently available to church leaders for equipping them with the biblical instruction and pastoral skills they need to lead the church into the future."

"An elephant on chicken legs." What do you think Jesus would do with that image of his church? And what counsel would Jesus give North Americans about their river that is "two miles wide and two inches deep"? I think Jesus would tell us something today that sounds similar to the words he pronounced in an earlier time and place:

Go therefore and make disciples of all nations, baptizing them in the name of the Father and of the Son and of the Holy Spirit, and teaching them to obey everything that I have commanded you. And remember I am with you always, to the end of the age. (Matthew 28:19-20)

For discussion

a. Describe your favorite teacher from any period or place in your life: school, church, workplace, etc. Then discuss what it was that made that teacher so outstanding and memorable.

b. What is the relationship between "evangelism" and "teaching"? Are they complementary? In conflict? Apples and oranges? How did Jesus or the early church work at this issue? Give concrete examples from the New Testament accounts.

c. Discuss where teaching happens in the life of your local congregation. Is there enough of it happening in light of what Jesus is calling for in Matthew 28? Are members in your congregation taught to obey "everything that [Jesus has] commanded"? How could the teaching program of your congregation be improved to better equip members for faithful kingdom living?

SESSION 6

Missional practices: Congregational life before the watching world

Linford Stutzman

IMMANUEL MENNONITE CHURCH in Harrisonburg, Virginia, was started in 1991 by a diverse group of missional dreamers. Many had either served in mission and service assignments overseas or lived in the Northeast Community of Harrisonburg, a neglected and socially, ethnically, and economically diverse neighborhood.

Decades before, mission-minded visionaries, some from local Mennonite congregations, others from Eastern Mennonite University—both students and facility—had begun such outreach ministries in the Northeast Community as vacation Bible school, home meetings, and Sunday school. Eventually a small Mennonite church emerged from this mission.

By the end of the 1980s the Northeast Community had become, at least in public opinion, notorious for its problems of drugs, gangs, and violence. By 1990 the small Mennonite mission church was deeply divided by differing views of its mission. What should the church be doing?

On one hand, some enjoyed the feeling of family, the close fellowship, the informality of a small, nontraditional congregation, a "contrast community" to the more wealthy, large, established

Mennonite congregations in the Harrisonburg area.

On the other hand, others were eager to be engaged in sharing the good news in a way that would address the social and spiritual needs within the neighborhood and to attract new members from the community into the congregation. A vision for a "contrast community" began to develop. By1990 a new congregation was formed with a commitment to reconciliation in a racially, socially, and economically divided neighborhood.

On top of a hill in the Northeast Community were the ruins of an old swimming pool. It was a crumbling, overgrown, debris-filled monument to the official end of segregation in the 1960s when, after the Civil Rights Act, blacks were allowed to use the large municipal swimming pools in the city of Harrisonburg. It was hoped that at this new church would become a "light on the hill." It would be another visible sign of the hope of God's kingdom in the Northeast Community.

The choice to build a church building on the old swimming pool site, to open a day-care center, and to participate in Neighborhood Watch and prayer walks, was noticed by everyone. These included the drug dealers on the adjacent street corner, local politicians, community activists and leaders, local church leaders, and everyone else. Some were pleased; others were not. (Two bullet holes adorned the window above the front door almost as soon as the construction was completed.) Ten years later, Immanuel has become a "city on a hill," not because of its location but because of its actions.

Biblical texts

John 13:31-35

> [31] When he had gone out, Jesus said, "Now the Son of Man has been glorified, and God has been glorified in him. [32] If God has been glorified in him, God will also glorify him in himself and will glorify him at once [33] "Little children, I am with you only a little longer. You will look for me, and as I said to the Jews, so; now I say to you, 'Where I am going, you cannot come.' [34] I give

you a new commandment, that you love one another. Just as I have loved you, you also should love one another. [35] By this everyone will know that you are my disciples, if you have love for one another."

Matthew 5:13-16; 6:10

[13] "You are the salt of the earth; but if salt has lost its taste, how can its saltiness be restored? It is no longer good for anything, but is thrown out and trampled under foot.

[14] "You are the light of the world. A city built on a hill cannot be hid. [15] No one after lighting a lamp puts it under the bushel basket, but on the lampstand, and it gives light to all in the house. [16] In the same way, let your light shine before others, so that they may see your good works and give glory to your Father in heaven."

[10] "Your kingdom come.
Your will be done,
on earth as it is in heaven."

Context—Where are we?

Let's imagine Jesus on top of the steep hill that rises above the north end of the Sea of Galilee. From there he could look to the south and east to the area of Decapolis across the lake. Above the city on a hill, typical of the pre-Roman cities of the area that were built on hills for protection, was the town of Kursi. Built on a hill, rising above the lake, it was visible for miles, day and night, all year round.

Jesus, having grown up in the small town of Nazareth, was thoroughly culturally and religiously Jewish, well versed in the law and the various interpretations and applications to every part of life. The Sermon on the Mount, as well as the teachings of Jesus throughout the Gospel, can be viewed as both connecting to and contrasting with his own Jewish religious culture.

What is less obvious reading the Gospels is that Jesus was also acquainted with his pagan neighbors in Galilee. He knew the cities built throughout the region such as Caesarea Philippi at the foot of Mount Herman to the north, a city dedicated to the worship of the Greek god Pan. Jesus had likely passed through the modern Roman city of Scythopolis on the route between Nazareth and Jerusalem and had seen the magnificent temples, palaces, and theaters. Jesus grew up with Romans living in the area, soldiers who had put down roots and become permanent residents of Galilee. They added pluralistic color and a pagan challenge to the Jewish world of Jesus. Although little is mentioned in the Gospels, Jesus was likely familiar with the glittering attraction of the pagan gods and the cities that demonstrated their power within the Roman Empire as well as with those within Judaism.

"You," Jesus, in essence, told his listeners on the hill above Galilee, "are to be like the city on the hill," built in contrast to the pagan cities of the Romans, visible within paganism, within the cultural landscape, yet dynamically distinct, drawing both positive and negative attention.

The followers of Jesus were also to demonstrate the missionary life of God's kingdom. Their life was to visibly and publicly contrast with the reactionary or defensive variety of Jewish religious cultural options, such as the Zealots or the Pharisees that probably appealed to the Jewish rural villagers in Galilee. The followers of Jesus were to demonstrate and proclaim the good news in ways that were in contrast with the prescriptions of the scribes, teachers, as well as the Sadducees who were based in Jerusalem. This "city on a hill," over which Jesus wept, had made little impact on the powerful paganism that had invaded the region.

Jesus was describing how his followers, the church, could make the good news of the reign of God dynamic, visible, relevant, powerful, and attractive. The good news stood in dynamic contrast to the promises of paganism of the Roman Empire. It was equally in contrast to the traditional Jewish village culture. Jesus was the original, authentic light of God's reign in the context of the religious Jewish world and the pagan Roman Empire. He embodied and proclaimed the message of the good news of the reign of God in public, and told his followers to do the same.

All local congregations in North America have much in common with the Jewish villages and cities of Galilee. We yearn for the days when pagan influence was more remote. We are tempted to react negatively against the pagan promises or to withdraw into self-protective enclaves. Neither option reduces the effects of paganism. Through technology, the lives of Christians are increasingly invaded and shaped by the powerful pagan promises that appear to be "good news." These promises of immediate rewards of health, wealth, security, prosperity, fame, beauty, and power are the same ones promised by Greco-Roman paganism that had invaded Galilee. It was a culture that glittered, beaconed, and welcomed the church of Jesus to join the city just as the pagan cities had attracted many Jews to become hellenized. We, like Jesus, are also surrounded by the failure of these promises. We live with the negative consequences of believing them.

Our congregations may have been located safely away from the pagan cities at one time, but urbanization, the Internet, and cable TV have made both paganism and Christendom our neighbors. The temptation for the church is to blend the good news into the pagan or religious molds, to attack paganism like the Zealots, or to preserve our distinctive culture like the Pharisees. The city on a hill does not seem to fit the new landscape. If we are not tempted to move figuratively to the new cities on the plain, we are at least tempted to lower the lights of our city in order to avoid attracting the negative attention of our powerful neighbors. The contrast between the city on a hill with the powerful, attractive, wealthy, promising cities of the Roman Empire and the ineffective little dark villages of the Jewish peasants is the picture of the church today. It is visible, contrasting, alive, relevant, powerful, and hopeful to the marginalized. It threatens the status quo in today's world of pagan promises, pop spirituality, and self-preserving cultural religion.

Gospel—What is God doing?

Jesus was God's good news. Jesus made the good news of the reign of God visible, present, attractive, powerful, threatening, and relevant in his teaching, his relationships, his healing, and his forgiveness. Both the public teaching and the public demonstration of the reign of God contrasted and connected with the Jewish-pagan context of Palestine.

Jesus was the light of the world, the light on the hill. In Galilee, his healing and hope, his miracles and teaching, his relationship to others, and in his love that led him to the cross made the good news visible. Jesus invited his disciples and followers to do the same thing.

Church—How is God calling and sending us?

God is calling and sending us to participate in God's mission in the world. What can we learn from this text to give us direction to fulfill this task in our own neighborhoods?

Worship and confess Christ openly. The worship at Immanuel is a celebration of the finished work of Jesus in his life, death and resurrection. It worships in anticipation of the coming kingdom. Immanuel is unapologetically and unashamedly committed to glorifying Jesus explicitly, repeating for the faithful and the seekers the good news of Jesus' life, death, resurrection, and return.

The congregational and worship leaders represent unity around Jesus and diversity in every other area. Male and female, young and old, rich and poor, formally educated and less educated, single parents and married people together embody and demonstrate the reality of the good news of the gospel every time the congregation gathers to proclaim and praise.

Many Christians believe that the works of the kingdom are adequate in making the good news of the kingdom known. They like to quote Francis of Assisi, who said, "Always preach the gospel, when necessary use words." Perhaps in the fourteenth century it may have been unnecessary to use words but in the twenty-first century it is *always* necessary.

Our culture glorifies those who do good, and will glorify the church when its good deeds, its good values, and its good qualities benefit society. But the goal of the church is not to be commended for its contribution to society. The highest goal is not even to attract members through its good ministries. Rather, it is to glorify Jesus in all that it does.

Worship and public confession of Jesus are both the foundation and the goal of missional engagement within our culture. Worship and public confession are absolutely necessary if the church is to remain a contrast society, because many groups, including all religious groups, advocate ethical behavior and do good deeds. It is the living Lord who makes the missional church distinct from both religious and pagan culture. Worship that celebrates before the world the finished work of Jesus and anticipates the coming kingdom is a powerful contrast to a culture trapped in the pagan promises of the present and the religious culture of the past.

For discussion

a. Is worship in your congregation a public confession and demonstration of Jesus as Lord in the past, present and future?

Actively connect the life of the congregation to the local context. When the pioneers of Immanuel Mennonite Church were testing the call and the vision to locate within the Northeast Community, they agreed to do two things. First, they researched the needs of the neighborhood in order to reach out in ministry once they had made the move. Second, they asked the residents *whether* they should start a new church in the area, and under what circumstances they would be welcome.

Several public meetings were announced inviting the residents to meet with the Immanuel people. Over a period of months community leaders, local church members, public officials, and many other residents of the Northeast met with the Immanuel group. They voiced their fears, hopes, and vision for a new church in their neighborhood.

A consensus emerged. Immanuel would be welcomed on several conditions. They should (1) work with the local churches already active in the community; (2) build a building that could be used for a variety of community initiatives; and (3) start a day-care center for children that everyone in the neighborhood could afford.

After the Immanuel group agreed to these conditions, a town meeting was announced for all interested people. They would vote whether Immanuel should locate in the community. After intense debate for and against, a vote was taken. By a narrow margin the majority invited Immanuel to locate in the community.

While not all congregations work toward his kind of consensus, all congregations have opportunities to connect their congregational life with the community in a way that shapes their ministries. Jesus is the example for connecting. Seldom did he minister to persons without listening to their expectations, hopes, needs, fears, and longings. While not limiting his actions entirely to what people wanted, Jesus directly connected his acts of the kingdom to the people's expectations.

For discussion

a. What are people asking the followers of Jesus to do in your community?

When the Great Commission is properly conceived as making disciples, it should then become apparent that disciple-making is a process that will continue until Christ returns. In other words, the Great Commission can never be fulfilled, *and we are doing a great disservice when we declare any part of the world to have been* reached.

—Engel and Dyrness, *Changing the Mind of Missions* (Downers Grove, Ill: InterVarsity Press, 2000) pp. 66-67.

Do good works publicly. Perform the life of the kingdom deliberately before the watching world. When the congregation was established in the Northeast Community one of its first activities was to join a much publicized (and heavily resisted) prayer walk/Neighborhood Watch program initiated by other local churches. Out-of-town drug dealers had claimed certain turf areas. These dealers did not appreciate any local interference with their business. The tension this generated, and its ultimate success was highly publicized in the local newspaper.

The church is called to be like Jesus in the world: to embody in public and to practice the good news of the kingdom in a way that is good for the community in which it exists, whether or not individuals join the church.

All the world's a stage, and all Christians are actors of the kingdom, "strutting and fretting their hour upon the world's stage," to paraphrase William Shakespeare. Jesus has given the congregation the role of acting out the good news of the kingdom before a watching world. The script is the teachings and actions of Jesus, especially the Sermon on the Mount. The congregation, as theater troupe of the kingdom, must rehearse the script in public until the roles are genuine demonstrations of the power, the relevance, and the goodness of the reign of God. How will everyone know that we are disciples of Jesus by our love to one another unless we demonstrate it in our public performances?

This is a frightening prospect, for our congregational life never seems to be ready to be played out before a skeptical, postmodern audience. Yet it is in the public rehearsals of the kingdom that Jesus' strength is portrayed in our weakness. If the congregation rehearses the script with the hope that when the congregation can perform the life of the kingdom flawlessly, the show may go public but it will never have an audience.

For discussion

a. What opportunities does your congregation have to publicly perform the life of the reign of God in your community?
b. Is your congregation a city on a hill, demonstrating the reality of the coming reign of God in relevant, powerful, and faithful ways in your local community? Jesus was the light of the world. All congregations where Jesus is glorified, where the coming reign of God is demonstrated before the watching world, can be like Jesus. Discuss how that can happen in your congregation.

SESSION 7

Dealing with resistance

Lois Barrett

WHEN THE BOULDER MENNONITE CHURCH in Colorado decided to give sanctuary to a conscientious objector in the Navy during the Gulf War, members knew it would not be a popular stand. The pastors started receiving harassing phone calls. Then one Sunday morning church members arrived to find red paint splashed against the front door of the church building.

That incident has not stopped the peace witness of the Boulder congregation. Their building is near the University of Colorado campus. In more recent years when there have been riots on the "hill" (a shopping area where students and storeowners have clashed), a Christian Peacemaker Team from the congregation has gone to the "hill" to talk to shop owners, students, and police as well as to be a peaceful presence.

Biblical texts

John 17:14-24

[14] "I have given them your word, and the world has hated them because they do not belong to the world, just as I do not belong to the world. [15] I am not asking you to take them out of the world, but I ask you to protect them from the evil one. [16] They do not belong to the world, just as I do not belong to the world. [17] Sanctify them in the truth; your word is truth. [18] As you have sent me into the world, so I have sent them into the world. [19] And for their sakes I sanctify myself, so that

they also may be sanctified in truth. [20] I ask not only on behalf of these, but also on behalf of those who will believe in me through their word, [21] that they may all be one. As you, Father, are in me and I am in you, may they also be in us, so that the world may believe that you have sent me.
[22] The glory that you have given me I have given them, so that they may be one, as we are one. [23] I in them and you in me, that they may become completely one, so that the world may know that you have sent me and have loved them even as you have loved me. [24] Father, I desire that those also, whom you have given me, may be with me where I am, to see my glory, which you have given me because you loved me before the foundation of the world.

Romans 12:14-21

[14] Bless those who persecute you; bless and do not curse them. [15] Rejoice with those who rejoice, weep with those who weep. [16] Live in harmony with one another; do not be haughty, but associate with the lowly; do not claim to be wiser than you are. [17] Do not repay anyone evil for evil, but take thought for what is noble in the sight of all. [18] If it is possible, so far as it depends on you, live peaceably with all. [19] Beloved, never avenge yourselves, but leave room for the wrath of God; for it is written, "Vengeance is mine, I will repay, says the Lord." [20] No, "if your enemies are hungry, feed them; if they are thirsty, give them something to drink; for by doing this you will heap burning coals on their heads. [21] Do not be overcome by evil, but overcome evil with good.

In the world, but not of the world

The context of Jesus' prayer for his disciples in John 17 is his impending arrest and execution. Earlier Jesus had told his disciples, "If the world hates you, be aware that it hated me before it hated you. . . . Because you do not belong to the world . . . there-

Menno Simons, Dutch Anabaptist reformer, wrote in 1554: "The sixth sign [by which the church of Christ may be known] is the pressing cross of Christ, which is borne for the sake of His testimony and Word. Christ says unto all His disciples, Ye shall be hated of all nations for my name's sake. Matthew 24:9. All that will live godly in Christ Jesus shall suffer persecution. 2 Timothy 3:12. . . . O Lord! Dear Lord! Grant that the wrathful dragon may not entirely devour Thy poor little flock, but that we, by Thy grace, may in patience conquer by the sword of Thy mouth; and may leave an abiding seed, which shall keep Thy commandments, preserve Thy testimony, and eternally praise Thy great and glorious name. Amen, dear Lord. Amen."

—*The Complete Writings of Menno Simons* (Herald Press, 1956) pp. 741-42.

fore the world hates you. . . . If they persecuted me, they will persecute you; if they kept my word, they will keep yours also" (15:18-20). At the end of Jesus' last discourse (John 14–16), the disciples say in essence, "Now we understand! Now we believe!"

Now Jesus prays for them. He begins, "Father, the hour has come" (17:1). He is soon to be killed. Those who follow Jesus are likely to share his fate. The disciples are to be sent out into the world, but they "do not belong to the world." They behave according to different standards from the world's standards. Therefore "the world has hated them" (17:14). They need protection from the evil one.

Likewise in Romans 12, the assumption is that there are people around who persecute. There are those who do evil against others. There is difficulty in living peaceably with some people. People are tempted to take revenge. There are enemies. And there is evil in the world.

For discussion

a. Why do you think the world hates people who march to a different drummer? What are the things that tempt us to take revenge?

God's purpose—that the world may believe

God's purpose, to be fulfilled in part through the disciples of Jesus, is "that the world may believe" that God has sent Jesus, the Messiah. The gospel, the good news, is that Jesus has given the disciples God's word (John 17:14). God will protect them from the evil one (17:15). God sanctifies, or consecrates, them (17:17-19). God makes the church one (17:22). All this, so that "the world may know that you have sent me and have loved them even as you have loved me," Jesus prays to God (17:23).

What does it mean that God will sanctify, or consecrates, the followers of Jesus? In ordinary English, we might say that God makes them holy. To be holy is to be set apart for God's service. It means to be different, for God's sake. It means not belonging to the world. It means living the truth, keeping Jesus' word, being faithful to the covenant with God—and thus not being conformed to the world (see Romans 12:2).

In the Old Testament, priests were consecrated. Prophets were consecrated. God tells Jeremiah, "Before you were born I consecrated you; I appointed you a prophet to the nations" (1:5).

Note that in John 17 and Romans 12, it is not special individuals who are consecrated; it is the whole community of believers. This is not about individual sainthood, but the holiness of the community that is set apart to participate in God's mission in the world. This holiness involves having an intimate relationship with God and with Jesus—"I in them and you in me, that they may become completely one" (17:23). They will even share God's glory (17:22)! This is not so that followers of Jesus can feel more comfortable or have their needs met or have a spiritual high—and stop there. This sanctification of the church is so that the world might believe.

For discussion

a. What is God's good news in John 17?
b. How does this text call us to change?
c. How does this text help us understand the church as consecrated to God's purpose in the world?

Overcoming evil with good

So how are people of the sanctified church, sharing God's glory, to behave in the world? They are in the world, but they are not to act like the world. They are in the world, but they do not belong to the world. And the world is sometimes hostile to them.

In John 17:18, Jesus prays, "As you have sent me into the world, so I have sent them into the world." How did Jesus deal with various forms of evil? He cast out unclean spirits. He healed people of diseases. He preached repentance and the inbreaking of the reign of God, to set things right.

And when he was arrested, Jesus did not resist violently. When Peter tried to fight back with a sword, Jesus told him, "Put your sword back into its sheath. Am I not to drink the cup that the Father has given me?" (John 18:11). Jesus told Pilate, "My kingdom is not from this world. If my kingdom were from this world, my followers would be fighting to keep me from being handed over to the Jews. But as it is, my kingdom is not from here" (18:36).

Romans 12 gives a succinct list of instructions on how to behave in the world when you don't belong to the world: Bless those who persecute you; bless and do not curse them. Live in harmony with one another. Do not be haughty or pretending to be something you are not. Do not repay anyone evil for evil. Leave vengeance up to God. Let God be the one who defends you. You can't control others' behavior, but if it is possible, so far as it depends on you, live peaceably with all. Do not be overcome by evil, but overcome evil with good.

This list of instructions goes counter to much that the world teaches us. Most cultures in North America tell us to "fight fire with fire." Counteract violence with more violence. Punish those who attack us.

In contrast, the New Testament tells us that evil cannot be overcome by evil. Evil can only be overcome with good. Hate cannot cancel out hate; only love can overcome hate. For this we have Jesus as example.

This is not only to be the private behavior for Christians, but their public behavior. Christians are to "take thought for what is noble *in the sight of all.*" Others are watching the church. Will they behave like Jesus? Will they really feed their enemies rather than take revenge?

Jesus is sending the church into the world to carry out the same mission for which God sent Jesus into the world (John 17:18). The church is both to demonstrate the gospel and to speak the gospel—so that the world may believe in Jesus, the Messiah sent from God. This missional church conducts its life together in the sight of all and speaks God's word of truth—so that the world may believe. As God sent Jesus into the world, so Jesus is sending us.

For discussion

a. How does God want the church to respond to hostility?
b. How does overcoming evil with good and blessing enemies put the church at odds with the way the world does things? How is acting peaceably a sign to the world of the reign of God?
c. How is the internal life of the congregation an external message about what God wants for the world?
d. How is God sending your congregation or group as Jesus was sent?

Mission-Focused Congregations: A Bible Study

The purpose of this study is (1) to provide a fuller definition of missional church through careful examination of the New Testament and (2) to inspire congregations and small groups to see themselves as missional, both in what they do and in who they are.
—*Introduction*

God is the first missionary. God works in many ways, but especially through the saving presence of Jesus Christ. While the church is invited in, it is not the author of mission. To be invited, as a co-worker, into the reconciling work of God is a very high honor for the church.
—*Robert J. Suderman, Session 1*

Because forgiveness and peacemaking are so closely tied to mission, we cannot be effective ambassadors for Christ unless we ourselves have been reconciled to God.
—*J. Nelson Kraybill, Session 2*

In a church in Minneapolis, immigrants from once-warring Ethiopia and Eritrea worship in the same pew. In Markham, Illinois, a congregation intentionally includes black and white members. In a church in Kansas, an ex-con and his young daughter become practically family members of a middle-class couple. These are missional churches in action!
—*Lois Barrett, Session 3*

The community of faith takes on a lifestyle that reflects its intention to be a community of equality, solidarity, and generosity, a community that shocks people because of the form of its obedience to its Master. Little by little, they become a demonstration of justice in the midst of a corrupt world.
—Gilberto Flores, Session 4

When we have finally reached the end of the road with all the questions and excuses our small minds can muster, Jesus comes to us—as he did to that first band of disciples—with words that call into question our limited cultural understandings and assumptions and invite us to reconsider the radical nature of his claim on our lives.
—James Krabill, Session 5

Worship and public confession of Jesus is both the foundation and the goal of missional engagement within our culture. It is the living Lord who makes the missional church distinct from both religious and pagan culture.
—Linford Stutzman, Session 6

Christians are to "take thought for what is noble *in the sight* of all." Others are watching the church. Will they behave like Jesus? Will they really feed their enemies rather than take revenge?
—Lois Barrett, Session 7

This resource builds on the conviction that only rigorous biblical formation will shape the church for its missional calling. In stimulating and provocative ways it poses questions that unpack the Scripture's transforming power. I heartily commend it for study and imitation as we learn about how to do "missional interpretation" of the Bible.
—Darrell L. Guder, Henry Winters Luce Professor of Missional and Ecumenical Theology, Princeton Theological Seminary

Here is a clear call to Mennonite congregations in North America to emerge from our comfort zones and to engage our society as active participants in God's compassionate mission in his world. The prophetic and missional stance envisioned in these

pages should stimulate our compassion and increase our capacity to imagine God's saving agenda. It will restore to the church its intended relevance as God's communities of mission in the world. In this process, hope will most certainly be revived, not only for the world, but for the church as well.
—*John Driver, Goshen, Indiana, veteran Mennonite educator, teacher, writer, and missionary in Latin America and other areas*

"What do you mean by 'missional church'?" people ask. We need a resource that helps us rediscover a missional imagination by connecting biblical content with our incredibly changing world. These Bible studies do just that! Here is an excellent tool for traveling further into God's intentions for the church.
—*Al Roxburgh, North Vancouver, British Columbia, president, The Missional Leadership Institute*

Mission-Focused Congregations is a most timely resource. It furnishes a clear biblical framework for understanding the nature and purpose of the church. It encourages the congregation to cultivate a lifestyle aligned with God's mission in the world. This Bible study addresses the fundamental need every congregation has: to attune itself continuously to being the witnessing-serving body of Christ in the world today.
—*Wilbert R. Shenk, teacher, Fuller Theological Seminary, Pasadena, California*

This study does not tell us "how" as much as "why" we should take the call to be a missional church seriously. Use the study to inform, but even more, to inspire—to help us tap into energy that God has given us to be a faithful church.
—*Jim Schrag, executive director, Executive Board, Mennonite Church USA, Newton, Kansas*

This study is equally rooted solidly in the scriptures and in the reality of life. While written for group discussion, this material may also serve as a guide for personal reflection. It is a resource for preparing sermons or lectures on the purpose of the church.
—*Dan Nighswander, general secretary, General Board, Mennonite Church Canada, Winnipeg, Manitoba*